# Scrapbooking Your Vacations

MONEY

SINGAPORE

Cayma

Sea

EXCURSION (EKS·KUR´·ZHEN)  1. A SHORT JOURNEY SPECIFICALLY FOR PLEASURE

Wisdom

Kathmandu, Nepal

NEPAL

Hindu woman with grandson

wearing tribal beads

# Scrapbooking Your Vacations
## 200 Page Designs

EXCURSION

Our Vacation

## by Susan Ure

Sterling Publishing Co., Inc.
New York

Chapelle, Ltd.:
    Jo Packham
    Sara Toliver
    Cindy Stoeckl

    Editor/Photo Stylist: Mackenzie Johnson
    Copy Editor: Marilyn Goff
    Staff: Kelly Ashkettle, Areta Bingham, Donna Chambers,
    Emily Frandsen, Lana Hall, Susan Jorgensen, Jennifer Luman,
    Melissa Maynard, Barbara Milburn, Lecia Monsen,
    Suzy Skadburg, Kim Taylor, Linda Venditti, Desirée Wybrow

Every effort has been made to ensure that all information in this book
is accurate. However, due to differing conditions, tools, and individ-
ual skills, the publisher cannot be responsible for any injuries, losses,
and/or other damages which may result from the use of the information in this book.

This volume is meant to stimulate craft ideas. If readers are unfamil-
iar or not proficient in a skill necessary to attempt a project, we urge
that they refer to an instructional book specifically addressing the
required technique.

Library of Congress Cataloging-in-Publication Data
Ure, Susan.
   Scrapbooking your vacations : 200 page designs / by Susan Ure.
      p. cm.
   "A Sterling/Chapelle Book."
   ISBN 1-4027-0819-X
   1.  Photograph albums. 2.  Photographs--Conservation and restoration.
3.  Scrapbooks.  I. Title.
TR465 .U74 2004
745.593--dc22
                              2003023619

10  9 8 7 6 5 4 3 2 1

Published in paperback in 2006 by Sterling Publishing Co., Inc.
387 Park Avenue South, New York, NY 10016
© 2004 by Susan Ure
Distributed in Canada by Sterling Publishing
c/o Canadian Manda Group, 165 Dufferin Street
Toronto, Ontario, Canada M6K 3H6
Distributed in the United Kingdom by GMC Distribution Services
Castle Place, 166 High Street, Lewes, East Sussex, England BN7 1XU
Distributed in Australia by Capricorn Link (Australia) Pty. Ltd.
P. O. Box 704, Windsor, NSW 2756, Australia

*Printed and Bound in China*
*All Rights Reserved*

Sterling ISBN-13: 978-1-4027-0819-0  Hardcover
        ISBN-10:1-4027-0819-X
        ISBN-13: 978-1-4027-4074-9  Paperback
        ISBN-10: 1-4027-4074-3

For information about custom editions, special sales, premium
and corporate purchases, please contact Sterling Special Sales
Department at 800-805-5489 or specialsales@sterlingpub.com.

# Table of Contents

Trip to Yellowstone

FALL

Jess with Phoebe the dog

3 Kids and their grandmother in a moose hat, in Yellowstone

# Introduction

Scrapbooking's popularity today is such that a myriad of books are available for learning basic "how to" techniques. The concept of this book is to showcase in gallery fashion one scrapbooking artist's creations. Our intention is more to inspire you than to teach you.

"I go to books and to nature as a bee goes to the flower, for a nectar that I can make into my own honey."

—J. Burroughs

The following pages are wonderful examples of artistically capturing vacation memories; retelling the stories, reliving the feelings, and re-creating the visual images through photographs and cutouts, captions and quotes. These images are then artfully designed in scrapbook page layouts. The work is exciting and filled with interest, not only for those who originally traveled but also for those who hope to and those who simply enjoy looking and learning.

A well-intended purpose for all of our scrapbook creations would be that the time and effort expended will result in pages of art that are worthwhile for years of repeated viewing by a variety of people, each receiving from the creations a very personal experience.

Each 9½″ x 11″ page was styled on a canvas of ripped-to-size, heavy-grade water-color paper. Layouts were designed as part of a loosely gathered collection from which pages might be easily separated for viewing. Dimensional elements of the designs often invite interactive reactions. Many of the pages could be converted into a framed wall display in matted or shadow-box format.

Some unique opportunities and challenges are initiated when you choose to work on a larger foundation paper. With that in mind, the artistic tips and materials lists found on the following pages offer valuable insights for design and layout selections and imaginative problem solving. Additionally, because the pages presented here have been embellished with many dimensional objects such as beads, brads, buttons, cords, charms, ribbons, tassels, and such, the archival quality has been compromised. The same is true for the use of adhesives. There are many types of glues and tapes, each serving different purposes for longevity, adhesion of varied surfaces, durability, and so on. Any use of adhesives should support your craftsmanship in an invisible manner. Pages such as those in this book may be safeguarded in clear protectors available for this type of scrapbooking. However, their creative purposes are markedly different than those scrapbooks prepared for archival storing. A variety of helpful suggestions throughout the text addresses these issues.

Despite the overall theme of "vacations" for the following pages, much individuality shouts out from the varied designs that chronicle the visited locales. The artist's personality is present in each creation, but is subtle in ways that are fun to discover as you study the collection more closely. There are some elements that are distinctly hers, yet she has carefully worked to expand upon her innate preferences. The result is an inviting, highly enjoyable, inspiring artistic journey taken through scrapbooked vacations.

Dear cousin's
I now take my pen
in hand to answ your letter
I got from you we are all
well and hope you are all the
same I have only had 8
teachers since school began
The first teacher name was
... the next Miss ...

BY AIR MAIL
PAR AVION

Rec Aug 17 1958

POSTMASTER,

AIR MAIL
6¢
U.S. POSTAGE

**European Experience:**
- England
- Ireland
- Germany
- France

- Spain
- Italy

...world is still deceived
...ornament...
...law, what plea so
...tainted and corrupt with
...gracious voice,
...obscures the show of evil?

"The quality of mercy is
not strained, it droppeth
as the gentle rain from
heaven upon the earth beneath
It is twice blest; It blesses
him that gives and him
that takes
'Tis mightiest in the
mightiest; it becomes the
throned monarch better
than his crown
His sceptre shows the
force of temporal power
...attribute to awe...
wherein doth...

# *Cheerio!*

Keepsakes from places visited can be displayed securely by using small florist's envelopes. Patterned vellum, creatively scalloped, frames this page and contrasts the base design. It's a finishing touch that surrounds and holds the design together.

# England

*Materials:*

Scrapbook Paper     Metallic Accent Piece
Patterned & Clear Vellum     Travel Keepsakes
Florist Envelope     Gold Brads
Floral Accent     Gold Floss

CHRISTMAS BOX
ST. NICHOLAS

The crown jewels

THE ROYAL COLLECTION

307 PORTOBELLO

Gold brads are an alternative to glue or double-sided tape for securing items. Travel keepsakes are held in a handcrafted semitransparent envelope made with vellum and brads. The repeated pattern links these two pages.

# Top o' the mornin' to you!

## Ireland

May you have:
A world of wishes at your
command
God and his angels close at
hand
Friends and family their
love impart,
And Irish blessings in your
heart.
Irish Blessing

A sense of place has been established by mounting this blarney stone photograph atop the flowing caption and quote. The lighthearted, personal mood is enhanced by a bulletin board background created with ribbons and gold brads.

*Ireland*

**Materials:**

Textured Scrapbook Paper     Book Cutouts
Picture Mats     Clear Vellum
Textured Ribbon     Floral Stickers
Victorian Calling Cards     Gold Brads
Decorative Crystal Buttons     Colored Chalks

Girls, close the doors now. Our part is over.
And you, happy pair. God bless you.
CATULLUS

Floral accents are easily cut from Victorian calling cards. The layout created by the ribbons contrasts artistically with the rectangular pictures. Scenes can be suspended within the diamond spaces and easily interchanged.

13

## Materials:

*Embossed Cardstock*
*Pressed Flowers*
*Lace Accents*
*Stamped Gift Tag*
*Recycled Note-card Papers*
*Silk Ribbon*
*Gold Cupid Charm*
*Heart Beads*

A travel journal motif may be fashioned by grouping together recycled note-card paper within a styled band. Enclosing it with ribbon and a charm adds the significance of a special keepsake. The band draws focus to the bordering photograph.

Pictures displayed need not always be your own shots. Stock photography, clip art, or cutouts from magazines and other sources can also be used.

## Materials:

| | |
|---|---|
| Embossed Cardstock | Floral Sew-ons |
| Handmade-paper Envelope | Gold Vellum |
| Travel Postcards | Decorative Buttons |
| Small Jewelry Bag | Silk Ribbon |
| Broken Glass Pieces | Gold Floss |
| Decorative Tissue Paper | Gold Brads |

Travel postcards may be displayed and protected within an envelope. To create a unique one, sew decorative buttons in a parallel line, then wrap gold floss around them to secure the flap. An interactive page is interesting in appearance and fun to enact.

Count these among your gifts:
the friendly morning sky,
the peaceful night,
and all the colors,
beauties,
splendors
of a living earth.

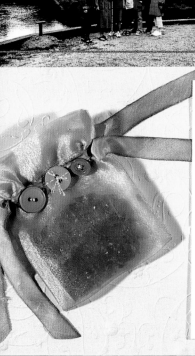

IRELAND

Be fearlessly imaginative with your embellishments. These pages include a decorated jewelry bag filled with green glass pieces and a fancifully written verse torn from tissue paper and attached with gold brads. The raised flowers are sewn on.

*Guten Tag!*

Angel, Adam & Nana, Rothenburg

Use a smaller picture mat placed over a larger photograph to spotlight specific portions within the picture yet not delete the surrounding scene. It's intriguing to catch just glimpses of the whole photograph.

# Germany

Materials:

Handmade Papers      Rosebud Accents
Embossed Picture Mats      Metallic Leaf Accents
Fossilized Leaves      Decorative Buttons

*Watch tower in Medieval Rothenburg*

The distinct handmade papers embrace the medieval mood. Their torn and layered appearance, in partnership with the fossilized leaves, also accents the photograph's season.

*Materials:*
*Colored Construction Papers*
*Stylized Scissors*
*Various Beads*
*Metallic Frame*
*Floral Stamp*
*Clear Vellum*

Use stylized scissors to create deckled edges for variety or to affect a particular design. The edges presented here mimic the lines of the architecture featured in the photographs. Repeating the cuts on just some of the edges, including the photographs, spotlights the design.

MEDIEVAL WALL, ROTHENBURG

FRESCO WALL IN BAMBERG

Background materials help to build a sense of depth when established in angles, layers, and colors. Angles definitely influence the mood. Tension may be added by slightly tilting horizontal photographs. Barely offsetting the elements of a page may create a sense of uneasiness.

## Materials:

**Textured Paper**
**Gold-leaved Tissue Paper**
**Colored Cardstocks**
**Colored Construction Papers**
**Clear Vellum**
**Stylized Scissors**

Colorful textured papers, layered with the light tones over the dark, draw attention to and enliven the framed photographs. The characteristics of the paper itself should also enhance similar features present within the photographs.

TOWN BUS BAMBERG, GERMANY

MEDIEVAL GARDEN, ROTHENBURG

Repeating decorative materials throughout a series of pages brings a sense of harmony to the collection. Using the same elements on corresponding pages but in diverse positions and with differing photos complements the styling of the pair and promotes overall continuity.

## Materials:

*Embossed Cardstock*
*Cord & Trim Elements*
*Decorative Buttons & Beads*
*Colored Wires*
*Clear Vellum*
*Sheer Ribbon*

The bright colors of the accent elements promote the cheerful mood of the photographs. Many different colors can be used together as long as they all have the same tonal feel (i.e. warm, cool, vibrant, earthy, rich, soft, etc.). The trim helps to frame the photograph and capture attention.

*Time out for lunch*

*Rothenburg*

*Arianne in Wonderland*
*Germany*

Captions may be used to expand upon the story told by the pictures. The captions themselves may contribute to the mood of a photograph simply by the way they are written. Therefore, thought should be given to the caption format. Handwritten inscriptions may add more of a personal touch; whereas, computer-generated fonts may be chosen to match particular styling. In some cases they are also cleaner and easier to read.

*Materials:*

**Hand-painted Paper**
**Handmade Tissue Paper**
**Textured & Clear Vellum**
**Colored Cardstock**
**Silk Ribbons**
**Cord & Trim Elements**
**Gold Floral Accents**

Adding distinct items such as hand-painted paper expresses significance. Unique trim and cord items placed around a photograph also direct attention to details and areas less apparent at first glance.

BAMBERG MUSEUM

THE MARKET PLACE

Interest may be established by combining textures, accents, and colors together in diverse arrangements. Care must be taken not to overwhelm a page. Make sure all elements used are complementary to one another and that angles are sparingly used. Combining elements that are in competition creates a sense of chaos and tension.

*Materials:*
**Fossilized Leaves
Ceramic Tiles
Garden Charms
Clear Vellum**

The ceramic tiles encourage focus on the architectural style of the photographed cottage. Placing the three leaves almost as a frame, softens the photograph's lines and also opens up the composition to questioning. It takes close study to discover the source for such accents.

A Medieval house in one of the oldest areas in Germany

Adam in Bamberg

The natural items featured here accentuate the picture's natural components. Placing the fossilized leaves as if springing forth from the scene, lifts the view and extends the artistic canvas. The photograph does not seem confined within its edges.

*Materials:*

*Colored Cardstock*
*Travel Keepsakes*
*Silver Clock Accents*
*Silver Floss*
*Silver Edged Gift Tag*
*Postcard Cutouts*
*Various Beads*

Colors carry their own inherent meanings and emotions. The rich, vibrant green shades of the pictured landscape inspired the dominantly green layout.

Including keepakes from the trip, such as travel tickets and documents, adds to the validity of an experience recorded in scrapbook form. Certain accents, such as the silver clocks, may be placed not only for decoration but as a visual springboard to signal memories which may have been forgotten.

# Parlez-vous Français?

The opulent theme of these pages was inspired by the stunning complexity of the subject matter. Lavish gift tags were made using different textures and embellishments. Intricate detail was also added by rubber-stamping on top of the fabric.

## France

*Materials:*

Patterned Papers     Decorative Buttons & Beads
Embossed Silver Strips     Alphabet Stickers
Cord & Trim Elements     Assorted Fabrics & Ribbons
Various Gift Tags     Heirloom Brooch
Gold Cherubs     Metallic Photo Corners

Metallic photo corners were used to mimic the appearance of a tag and the embossed silver strips at opposing edges of the page continue the carved richness of the settings.

Scrapbook Papers
Handmade Tissue Paper
Vintage Photograph
Cord & Trim Elements
Gold Tassels

Themed Stickers
Sheer Ribbon
Manila Envelope
Journal Entry
Metallic Photo Corners

A mood of French history and elegance is established through the choice of paper and accents. The busy composition is successful because all of the details connect and contribute to the desired sense of time and place. Vertical lines framing the top and bottom announce continuity and imply an ongoing story.

Une Pensée De Paris

Honeymoon in Paris April 2, 1933

Samuel R. & Elsie Thomas Cook

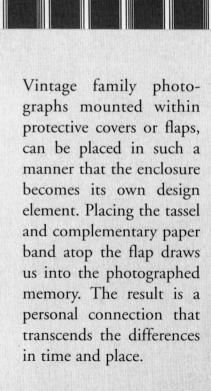

Vintage family photographs mounted within protective covers or flaps, can be placed in such a manner that the enclosure becomes its own design element. Placing the tassel and complementary paper band atop the flap draws us into the photographed memory. The result is a personal connection that transcends the differences in time and place.

## Materials:

Embossed Cardstock          Plastic Pouch
Scrapbook Papers            Themed Stickers
Checkered Ribbon            Metallic Photo Corners
Handmade Tissue Paper       Colored Brads
Heirloom Charm Bracelet     Clear Vellum

Personal possessions with significant meanings add to the nostalgia and importance of a scrapbook page. However, care must be taken to protect these delicate treasures. An heirloom charm bracelet is displayed by securing it in a transparent plastic pouch, allowing it to be admired as well as protected.

FOR PARIS IS A SUM TOTAL. PARIS IS THE CEILING OF THE HUMAN RACE. THIS ENTIRE PRODIGIOUS CITY IS AN EPITOME OF DEAD AND LIVING MANNERS AND CUSTOMS. HE WHO SEES PARIS SEEMS TO SEE ALL HISTORY THROUGH THE SKY AND CONSTELLATIONS IN THE INTERVALS.

-VICTOR HUGO

PARIS CIRCA 1922

France

Black-and-white photographs are fascinating variations for scrapbook pages. They add interest and artistic diversion. Dramatic color contrasts can be achieved with great impact on the mood and message. Red edging and spots of color stand out strikingly. Appropriately, the Victor Hugo quote speaks of Paris as a sum total.

Create interest with the repetition of design components such as shapes and colors. Simplistic placement of the pinwheel accents and the use of complementary colors reflects and enhances the repetitive geometric shapes within the photographs.

ARC DU DEFENSE PARIS

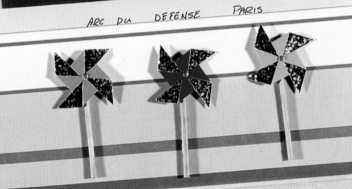

The use of contrasting colored lines draws attention to the similar composition and detail found within the featured photographs. The crocheted colored squares mimic the geometric nature of the pictures.

Changing of the Guard, Versailles

## Materials:

Colored Rice Papers
Gold-leaved Tissue Paper
Cord & Trim Elements
Floral Accent Piece
Princess Cutout
Various Miniature Gift Tags
Alphabet Stamps
Decorative Buttons & Beads
Rosebud Accents

Blend the color and texture of background papers to complement each other as well as to enhance the photographs placed on them.

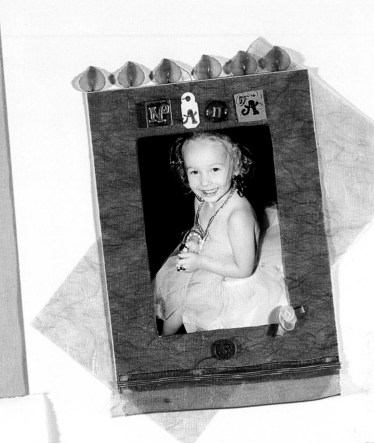

The vibrant colors help to emphasize the bright smiles of the little girl pictured. Photographs used need not always be of landmarks. Snapshots taken of family members at memorable moments make the page very special on a personal level.

*Materials:*

Colored Cardstock
Scrapbook Papers
Fabric Mesh
Colored Vellum
Die-cut Lettering

Beach-themed Die-cuts
Gold Starfish Charm
Colored Eyelets
Small Beads
Adhesive Pop-dots

Surf Sand Sun

Dynamic snapshots demand attention and it is best to place them in a layout that is subtle in design. This allows the pictures to speak for themselves. You can easily imagine words spoken in each of the above scenes.

# Olé, olé!

The placement of decorative elements on a page creates a certain hierarchy of importance. Pay attention to what grabs your eye first. Here, the impact of the photographs and title, have priority over the beach themed die-cuts.

*Materials:*

Handmade Paper      Area Map
Fabric Mesh      Various Beads
Metallic Alphabet Tiles      Pasta Accents
Various Gift Tags      Paint Swatches
Floral Die-cuts      Miniature Bell

On pages that need labeled identification, create lettering that ties into the theme. Here, it is similar to Italian tiles. The charming variances in size and shape match the look of the locale.

# *That's amore!*

A composition made three-dimensional invites entry into the scenes. Add small objects which extend the action toward you, as does the miniature bell attached at the apex of the building photographed.

## Materials:

Patterned Paper
Handmade Paper
Silver Vellum
Dried Leaves
Pressed Grapes
Wax Seals & Stamp
Metallic Tiles w/ Sayings
Silverware Charm

An alluring option for page design is to use various stamps on hot-wax seals. The seals offer historical perspective as well as provide an innovative way of attaching photographs to the scrapbook page.

Photographs mounted among specially dried and preserved items, such as these grapes from an Italian vineyard, trigger vacation memories. The inclusion of a visited region's actual resources makes the page educational and informative, as well as nostalgic.

## Materials:

| | |
|---|---|
| Embossed Cardstock | Various Gift Tags |
| Gold-leaved Tissue Papers | Fossilized Leaf |
| Embossed Paper Strips | Tussy-Mussy |
| Textured Pearlized Paper | Pressed Flowers |
| Assorted Fabrics & Ribbons | Feathers |
| Decorative Buttons & Beads | Gold Cherubs |
| Cord & Trim Elements | Gold Floss |

The ornate architecture was inspiration for the lavish gift tags created to adorn these designs. Surprising combinations of items are found within the tags, and form a delicate balance to the simple anchors, such as the gold cherubs and brief captions.

Tilting the photographs and some of the background materials signals excitement and wonder. It is especially appropriate here that the photograph of the Tower of Pisa leans.

## Materials:

*Rice Paper*
*Textured & Clear Vellum*
*Silver Frame*
*Tassels*
*String*
*Silver Eyelets*

Feelings may be conveyed simply by the inclusion of a related item. For example, the clothesline created above the picture places you into the scene and you more fully sense the lifestyle portrayed.

*View from our hotel*

*Venice*

The artistic placement of the green tassels draws the eye upward as if to the top of the building featured in the photograph. Such devices allow a scrapbook page to tell a story rather than merely display a picture.

*Life on the second story*

## *Materials:*

*Handpainted Paper*
*Colored Construction Paper*
*Handmade Paper*
*Glass Shards*
*Ceramic Tiles*
*Tussy-Mussy*
*Metallic Photo Corners*
*Clear Vellum*

Glass shards in shades of blue reflect the water which fills the many canals of Venice. This image is exaggerated by the shades of blue in the background papers. The vertical cropping and framing of the picture also pulls in the sides of the scene and imposes a close, narrow reality.

*Bridge of Sighs*

*Our hotel in Venice*

CAMPO
S. MARIA NOVA

Aromatic, flower-laden verandas are emphasized and extended with dried flowers inside a tussy-mussy. It should be noted that delicate accents require cautious handling and even then, may need occasional replacement. The dried flowers seen here are laid out so they could be easily refurbished.

*Materials:*
**Textured & Clear Vellum**
**Travel Keepsakes**
**Wax Seals & Stamp**
**Black Floss**

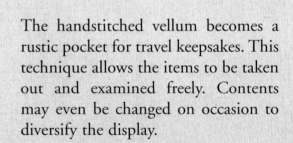

When appropriate, allow a single photograph to dictate a simple composition. The wax seal anchored photograph and ticket stub are meant to be the connected focus. Nothing else is intended to intrude or overwhelm the empty spaces. Less truly can be more.

The handstitched vellum becomes a rustic pocket for travel keepsakes. This technique allows the items to be taken out and examined freely. Contents may even be changed on occasion to diversify the display.

*Materials:*
**Corrugated Paper**
**Copper Mesh**
**Handmade Paper**

Roof tiles in Venice

The calligraphy and scrolling of the copper mesh augment the historical significance of the location pictured. The effect is as if we stand on a corrugated metal roof looking down on a narrow dark alleyway.

Venetian Canal

Some materials lend themselves to different alterations. Experiment with the limitations of various resources. For example, paper or tissue can be torn and crumpled up to produce textures. Copper mesh, normally thought of as stiff and unyielding, can be softened by rolling the edges around a pencil. Uncharacteristic effects form a sense of wonder and pleasant surprise.

*Materials:*

Scrapbook Papers      Paper Doilies
Colored Rice Paper      Silk Ribbon
Alphabet Stickers      Silver Brads
Alphabet Charms      Adhesive Pop-dots

These delightful, raised letters produced to connect the two pages under a leafy canopy of design were created using adhesive pop dots. The colored layers of stickers, papers, doilies, and ribbons comprise the title which connects with every photograph displayed. They also add exciting dimension. The diverse photographs are symbolically tied together.

## Materials:

*Souvenir Italian Marbled Paper*
*Handmade Papers*
*Pen & Ink Accents*
*Scroll Accents*
*Feather*
*Metallic Photo Corner*

These pages spotlight an actual paper product created by an Italian artisan. Photographs document the papermaking process. Along with being the subject of the pages, the handmade paper also works well as a decorative element.

*Italian Marbled Paper*

Possible uses of the handmade paper are implied by the placement of the pen, ink, and scroll embellishments. The page design has been kept simple to invite closer inspection of the artisans product.

*Florence*

*Materials:*

**Reproductions of Original Artwork**
**Gold-leaved Paper**
**Iridescent Cardstock**
**Metallic Frames**
**Bronze Brads**

Reproductions of original art pieces can be included for design and ambiance. They also serve as visual records of the known artistry and culture of the locations visited.

Reproductions showcased here provide an artist's interpretation of the areas visited. This alternate viewpoint fortifies the impressions presented through one's own travel pictures. Enclosing the captions in bold frames suggests an art gallery atmosphere.

43

## Materials:

*Patterned Papers*
*Iridescent Cardstock*
*Fabric Mesh*
*Various Gift Tags*
*Floral Die-cuts*
*Metallic Photo Corners*
*Metallic Frame*
*Garden Charms*

The choice of triangular patterned scrap-book paper reinforces the brick composition of the structures featured in the picture. Similar elements used repeatedly, such as the tag motif, links pages together regardless of the subject matter.

Geometric designs, usually thought to be strict and rigid, can actually be lively. The buoyant, springy feel of the grapevine die-cuts offsets the precisely patterned papers and helps give the layout character and variety. Their inclusion also augments the botanically themed photographs.

## Materials:

Gold-leaved Paper     Metallic Accents
Colored Cardstock     Italian Coins
Handmade Paper     Beaded Sew-on
Corrugated Paper     Tussy-Mussy
Gold Cherubs     Clear Vellum

The impression of the Italian coins is repeated the circular pattern found in the background paper and the gold piece which is placed centrally at the top. These round images contrast the horizontal waves of the corrugated paper and the photographed water, resulting in a pleasing balance.

A Venetian "Back Street"

"O sol o mio"

The time and effort spent photographing vacation highlights should also be expended when designing formats to record and share travel experiences. When that happens, the trip actually never need end.

Venice Gondola

## Materials:

Handmade Paper
Scrapbook Paper
Colored Cardstock
Cord & Trim Elements
Clear Plastic Envelope

Birdseed
Gold Bird Charm
Feather
Gold Cross Charm
Clear Vellum

*San Marco Cathedral*

Gold trim placed around the photograph visually strengthens the pictured cathedral, as does the gold cross charm. All elements contribute to the spiritual theme.

*San Marco Square, Venice*

Use design elements that support the photograph's story, mood, and/or action. It is magical to see a clear, plastic envelope filled with birdseed as an accent for the photograph of this popular pigeon and tourist attraction. The single feather punctuates the picture.

## Materials:

*Gold-leaved Paper*
*Scrapbook Paper*
*Gold Cardstock*
*Metallic Leaf Accents*
*Heirloom Cross Necklace*
*Miniature Mirrors*
*Gold Cherubs*
*Gold Trim*

Baroque, rococo, and Byzantine influences are found throughout these styled pages. The pictures feature religious icons which inspired the decorative embellishments and color scheme (i.e. the use of ornate gold pieces, mirrors, and regal tones of purple and gold).

Saint Maria

Religious influences in decor continue to be an integral part of Italy's architecture, especially in cathedrals. These influences are recognized in the inclusion of the cross necklace and the religious figures. Most of the accent elements are tile-like in their appearance and reflective of the intricate mosaics which decorate many of Italy's finest buildings.

Roma Basilica di Santa Pressede

African
Travel Safari:
• Kenya
• Masi Mara
   Reserve

• Kikonde
• Mombasa


Say
Cheese!

49

*Hakuna matata!*

# AFRICA

Kenya

Complex and diverse layering of varied patterns, textures, and colors reflect the complexity of Africa. It's also fun to use animal-print elements suggestive of the primal nature of Africa's inhabitants.

**Materials:**

Patterned Papers          Tin Lettering
Colored Construction Papers    Alphabet Stickers
Colored Rice Paper        Artificial Flowers
Scrapbook Papers          Moss
Animal-print Flannel      Palm Husk

*guarding crops*

The diorama effect of this intriguing design builds from the bottom up with the placement of grasses and moss in front of the photograph. The eclectic patterns work artistically because of the ethnic subject matter.

## Materials:

*Tie-dyed Paper*
*Handmade Papers*
*Colored Cardstock*
*Fabric Mesh*
*Souvenir Ethnic Beads*
*Alphabet Stickers*
*Magnetic Words*
*Silver Eyelets*
*Colored Thread*

Handmade and tie-dyed papers establish a realistic setting. The clear alphabet stickers used to label the action appear as water drops for a whimsical touch that matches the humor of the pictures.

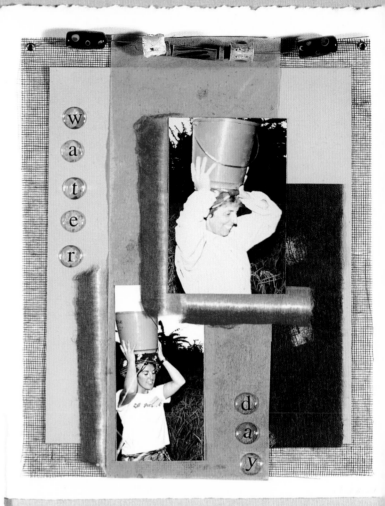

Black-and-white photographs contribute to a more complex page design. Use bright colors on some edges to make the photographs "pop" out. Stringing ethnic beads across the page, either vertically or horizontally, adds dimension and creatively exhibits souvenirs brought home.

*Materials:*

Patterned Paper
Corrugated Paper
Colored Cardstocks
Souvenir African Earrings
Beaded Sew-ons
Alphabet Stickers

Actual beaded earrings reflect the colorful nature and attire of the people visited. They are worn by one of the women pictured. The jewelry is a cultural keepsake chosen to be showcased in the layout.

Warrior dance

Masi Mara Reserve

The lettering, beadwork, and patterned paper also mirror the clothing worn in the photograph. Seasoned scrapbooking travelers knows to search for small artifacts as souvenirs. Beads, stones, twigs, buttons, and such, easily capture the essence of an experience. Adding authentic accents strengthens most compositions.

*Materials:*
**Textured Scrapbook Papers**
**Dictionary Clippings**
**Bird Stickers**

Mounting each photograph in offset fashion directs eye movement across the page. If you choose not to add narration, make certain each picture provides enough information to play off the other. A succession of photographs tells a story, much like the frames of a movie.

*Kenya,*
*Susan and*
*the Rhino!*

ADVENTURE (ad·ven´·cher) 1. a daring, hazardous undertaking 2. an unusual, exciting, often suspenseful experience

EXPERIENCE (ek·spir´·e·ens) 1. the act of living through an event 2. knowledge and skill gained through learning

[ ad·ven´·ture ]
*an unusual, exciting, often romantic experience*

DISCOVER (DI·SKUV´·ER) 1. TO BE THE FIRST TO FIND 2. TO LEARN OF THE EXISTENCE OF

The beauty of a good photo essay is that it necessitates very little verbal explanation. By selecting the right word or short phrase a total experience can be implied. The enlarged dictionary word grabs your attention, sets the mood for the photograph, and initiates an unspoken narrative.

*Materials:*

*Textured Paper*
*Scrapbook Paper*
*Beige Cardstock*
*Pom-pom Thread*
*Alphabet Stickers*
*Dictionary Clippings*

A clever way of conveying thoughts or ideas, apart from handwriting them, is to use dictionary definitions. Many times the photographs speak for themselves, but by adding the definitions, you can direct the feel or mood you wish associated with them.

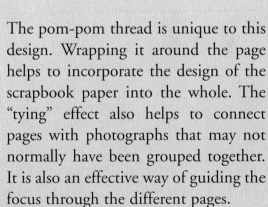

adventure (ad-ven´-cher) 1. a daring, hazardous undertaking 2. an unusual, exciting, often suspenseful experience

CHOICE HUMANITARIAN

2001

culture (kul´-cher) 1. the skills and arts, of a given people in a given period or civilization

The pom-pom thread is unique to this design. Wrapping it around the page helps to incorporate the design of the scrapbook paper into the whole. The "tying" effect also helps to connect pages with photographs that may not normally have been grouped together. It is also an effective way of guiding the focus through the different pages.

*Materials:*

Textured Papers      Metallic Alphabet Tiles
Woven-bamboo Paper      Newspaper Clippings
Textured Ribbon      Number Stickers
Terra-cotta Shards      Gold Shovel Charm

The terra-cotta shards highlight the earthy texture of these pictures. Numerous options are available for premade captions such as clippings from printed sources. The way in which the letters were cut and positions mimics that of the metallic alphabet tiles. Both are suggestive of building brick upon brick.

## Materials:

*Colored Cardstock*
*Slate Pieces*
*Fabric Mesh*
*Handmade Papers*
*Tile Swatches*
*Twine*
*Dried Grasses*
*Rubber Stamp w/ Phrase*

Background elements reflect the action of the photograph which is the hand-crafting of the bricks. The slate pieces chosen have an uneven appearance, much like handmade clay. Everything incorporated in a page design need not be authentic.

The brick wall in the picture seems lost because of the closer presence of the foreground group. Slate accents were used to divert the focus to the superbly handcrafted feat. The vertical design of the textured paper also pulls the view up to the wall.

*Materials:*
*Patterned Papers*
*Colored Cardstocks*
*Colored Construction Paper*
*Ceramic Tiles*
*Dictionary Clippings*
*Miniature Mirror Accents*
*Various Beads*
*Metallic Swirl Accents*

The playfulness and curiosity of the Kikonde children is wonderfully embraced in the vibrant colors and the included definition of fun.

DISCOVER

*Kikonde*

**fun** (fun)  1. lively, joyous play or playfulness; pleasure  2. a source of amusement    **explore**

[de´light]
to give great pleasure

*Fancy dancer*

Festive colors and lively patterns enhance the joyful celebration captured in the photograph. The merriment seems to spill out onto the rest of the page. The circular pattern of the background on one page and the square design on the other shouts diversity. Round and square elements are repeated randomly for a strong emphasis.

Asian
Adventure:
• India
• Nepal

• Thailand
• Japan

Picture
perfect!

# Treasured Traditions

A page can showcase many pictures of differing sizes if their contents connect in some way, i.e. subject, color, emotion, and so forth. The balance of their placement is very important but can be attained using items other than photographs.

# India

*Materials:*

Scrapbook Papers
Colored Cardstocks
Copper Gift Tags
Corrugated Paper
Clear Vellum

Jute & Raffia
Decorative Buttons
Linen Thread
Copper Brads
Copper Ribbon

Northern India
June 1967

"India is the cradle of the human race, the birthplace of human speech, the mother of history, grandmother of legend, and great grand mother of tradition. Our most valuable and most instructive materials in the history of man are treasured up in India only."
—Mark Twain

By using copper accents in complementary places, along with other rustic items such as jute and raffia, this page emotes the grandeur of India. The thought provoking quote is an intelligent accent.

# Trekking in the Himalayas.

Inclusion of an eye-catching informational brochure adds accurate details of a place. The beadwork and fabrics on the guide cover were inspiration for the page artifacts and embellishment.

**Nepal**

*Materials:*

| | |
|---|---|
| Colored Rice Papers | Decorative Buttons & Beads |
| Travel Brochure | Rubber Stamp w/ Asian Character |
| Area Map | Colored Photo Corners |
| Fan Accent | Clear Vellum |

Ascetic Priest

Temple Court Yard

The assorted handmade paper and tissue selections speak not only of the colors of Nepal, but also are symbolic of the culture, a simple lifestyle without cosmopolitan complexity; what you see is what you get.

### Materials:
**Colored Construction Paper**
**Colored Rice Paper**
**Clear Sticker**

Torn edges, used for the captions here, soften the hard lines of this page and balance the overall composition. The handwritten labels match the informal nature of the places pictured.

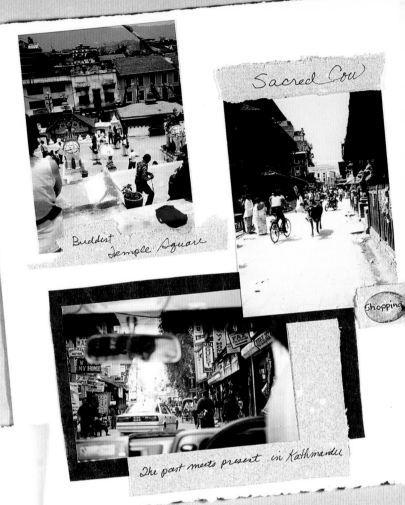

Buddist Temple Square

Sacred Cow

Shopping

The past meets present in Kathmandu

Kathmandu, Nepal.

Contrasting light and dark matting directs focus to the picture. Additionally, the angle of the wall points to the scene at the very center of the photograph. This simple image commands the page and our serious study of it. This dramatically framed page was created using only minimal materials.

## Materials:

*Rice Paper*
*Colored Vellum*
*Woven-bamboo Paper*
*Assorted Ribbons*
*Various Beads*

Including captions that identify places, actions, or people pictured helps to convey recollections and perceptions of locations visited. Artistically stylized captions add depth to the impact of the overall creation.

*Main Street, Kathmandu*

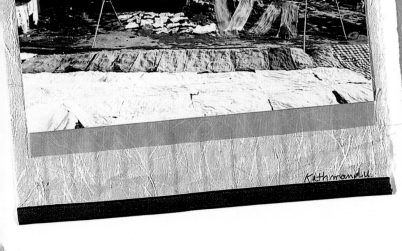

*Wash day*

*Kathmandu.*

Another way to draw deeper inspection and emotion is to build upon the message of a given scene. For example, the raw, frayed edges of the layered background papers match the action in the photograph. They help us to see what was originally experienced.

67

*Materials:*
*Handmade Papers*
*Cork Paper*
*Rubber Stamp w/ Asian Characters*
*Clear Vellum*

Old Kathmandu Temple

and grain harvest

Note how the large amount of ground space pictured in the lower right photograph pulls you toward the buildings at the back, as if you were walking right into them. This is an artistic example of good photographic composition.

Funeral Ghats

Buddhist Monk

Before entering the stage of designing scrapbook layouts, attention must be paid to creating pleasing pictures. Scenes that are well composed stand alone needing few embellishments for statement or style. Knowing how to crop pictures effectively is another valuable skill worth developing. Take photographs with purpose and intention. The scenes used here are excellent examples of powerful photography.

## Materials:

Handmade Papers
Assorted Tissue Papers
Colored Rice Papers
Gold Sheet Foil
Souvenir Beads
Clear Vellum
Clear Sticker

The torn edges of the assorted handmade papers mimic the frayed edges of the prayer flags as they are hung, waiting for the wind to carry the prayers heavenward. The colors are chosen to recreate the images of nature and the wild, windy world of Kathmandu.

Kathmandu Sacred Pig

Steps to Monkey Temple

365 Stairs

The Monkey Temple

in Kathmandu

To border these pictures only partially creates intrigue and interest. As with earlier pages, the fraying and tearing of the tissues and handmade papers corresponds to the weathering of the architecture showcased. The symbolic anchoring depicted with the beads seems to precariously hold the images in place. These pages work well as photographic essays.

*Materials:*

*Cork Paper*      *Yak Hair Yarn*
*Textured Paper*   *Metallic Floss*
*Various Beads*    *Silver Wire*
*Souvenir Beads*  *Clear Vellum*

Yaks in the Himalayas

Sacred rocks homage to Buddha

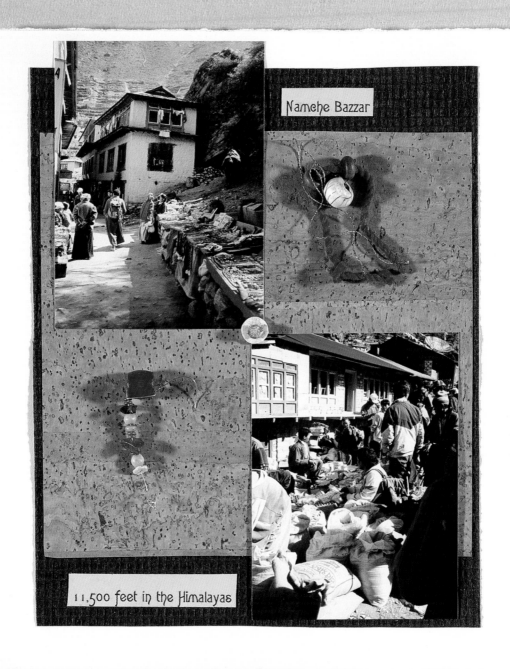

Namche Bazzar

11,500 feet in the Himalayas

Treasured souvenirs, such as the yak hair yarn and decorative beads, lend authenticity and wonder to these well balanced pages. From the burdened yaks and rocky cliffs to the busy marketplace bazaar the viewer is invited to take a deep breath and climb in.

*Materials:*

*Textured Paper*
*Textured Vellum*
*Silver Eyelets*
*Travel Keepsakes*

The general color compositions of these pages are very muted and neutral in tone, much like the landscapes photographed. For visual excitement, small bursts of color are skillfully placed, seemingly from nowhere, as if to say, "Wow, Look again!"

DINGBOCHE

The cropping of this distinctly vertical picture is fascinating. The layout capitalizes on the upward visual pull by accenting with the straight-edged stick and the textured lines of the background paper. Unique framing was accomplished with vellum folded back over the photograph and anchored with eyelets.

## Materials:

*Handmade Paper*
*Colored Rice Paper*
*Silver Beads*
*Silver Charm Bracelets*
*Metallic Photo Corners*
*Clear Vellum*

Accent papers and simple objects enrich the emotion of the picture's colors, textures, and subject matter. Rough edges, even overlapping the borders of the foundation page, add to the appeal of the page. Using a distant shot with a close-up personal view creates a sense of familiarity with the scene and curiosity about the passport and the person holding it so proudly.

Ang Temba our Sherpa

with Susan's passport

Our camp - Stupa and tents

In the mist of Namche Bazaar

Again, stepping outside the limits of the page is accomplished simply with the unevenly torn tissue. It expands the vista to an imaginative panorama of misty countryside. The placement of the charm bracelets also creates a line which contrasts the stone lines pictured, encouraging us to explore beyond what we think we see.

BANGKOK
The Grand Palace

tile work of Palace

The artistic elegance of this culture is showcased by leaving considerable white space from the foundation paper and using very simplistic accents. Appropriately, the captions are in calligraphy.

# Thailand

*Materials:*

**Dried Snake Grass**
**Pressed Flowers**
**Gold Sheet Foil**
**Funeral Papers**
**Small Twig**

Sacred Offerings

The natural accents are design statements which provide insight into this country's culture. Placement of the pressed flowers overlapping the more complex image makes an obvious statement, provoking introspection.

**Materials:**
*Funeral Papers*
*Gold & Silver Sheet Foil*
*Textured Vellum*
*Handmade Papers*
*Various Beads*
*Silver Wire*
*Small Twig*

These compositions are very stylized and the inclusion of symbolic pieces of art are meant to reflect travel experiences. Brief captions, limited artifacts, torn edges, and a touch of the metallic all combine with definite purpose.

WAT ARUN TEMPLE

*funeral paper*

As with previous pages, white space is utilized as an important component of this design. The initial choice to use heavy-grade watercolor paper, torn to size, for the foundation of the entire collection of scrapbook pages is well understood when viewing these compositions. The uneven lay and the rough edging are especially appropriate springboards for this locale and culture.

## Materials:

| | |
|---|---|
| Colored Rice Paper | Picture Mat |
| Handmade Papers | Pressed Onion Skin |
| Dried Seeds | Pressed Flowers |
| Raffia & String | Raised Leaf Stamp |
| Travel Brochure | Thai Coin |
| Handwoven Paper | Colored Wire |
| Handwritten Asian Characters | Small Twig |

Note how the picture is a small portion of the mood of this page; it merely begins the experience which is emotionally enlarged through the use of handmade papers and small artifacts from nature. The accent collection at the upper left of the page is an interesting balance to the Asian characters at the lower right.

THAI MARKET
in Chiang Mai

金 花 い も 大 紙

Thai Fruit

durian
mangosteen
lychee

Similar to the upper-left/lower-right balance noted above, this composition contrasts the English language interpretation with the native language caption. The page contains inviting and diverse lines created with various torn and cut papers, raffia, string, and wire. They seem to extend from a scene that reflects a western influence and the total effect builds curiosity.

# Materials:

Tie-dyed Paper      River Stone
Handmade Papers      Dried Seeds
Dried Snake Grass      Handwritten Asian Characters

typical house on chao phyraya river

life on the river

Both of these pieces, reflecting life on the river, successfully recreate the original scene. We seem to stand on a shore where we can smell the snake grass, feel the river stones underfoot, and hear the water flowing along. Tie-dyed paper becomes a colorful sky, dried seeds and grasses lend realism to the vegetation and the carefully torn handmade paper extends imaginatively from the river craft photographs. Wisely, the native writing reminds us where these images have taken us.

## Materials:

Handmade Paper      Raised Leaf Stamp
Textured Vellum      Elephant Charm
Hand-painted Paper      Various Beads
Dried Money Plant Leaves      Wooden Dowel
Handwritten Asian Characters      Clear Vellum

The exotic awe inspired by this photograph demands a stunning setting. The uniquely repetitive design created on the hand-painted paper resembles tiles built one upon another. This establishes an appropriate mood of strength and size. The dangling elephant charm is a perfect final touch as it imitates the sway of the elephant's trunk and the hanging vines of the jungle.

white elephant

Raft on Ping River

A page develops into an atmosphere as the chosen elements authentically combine to recreate a sense of place. From the vine-like wire-wrapped dowel suspending the scene at the top to the dried leaves and torn edging at the bottom, all of the components thematically connect so that you feel as though you are looking down on the raft from a tree or bamboo perch.

Cropping the photograph and empha-
sizing its vertical dimension invites you
to step forward onto the hanging bridge.
The lines of the the Asian writings and
the layered background papers draw this
scene toward us and secures our focus.

PING RIVER

MARY

An effective technique for a series of pages
similarly themed is to repeat a certain
accent, such as the hand-painted paper, in
each design. However, curiosity is aroused
when the placement is altered slightly in
each consecutive layout. By vertically alter-
ing the paper's position for this photograph,
the woman shown becomes more life-sized
and the thematic collection stays interesting.

# Moshi Moshi!

The creation of an origami-style, folded kimono in a size larger than the ones photographed, skillfully leads the viewer to a closer inspection of the scene. The handmade device seems to "open" the design.

# Japan

*Materials:*

Colored Cardstock     Asian Sticker
Patterned Papers     Photo Corners
Textured Paper     Gold Brads
Souvenir Japanese Brooch     Clear Vellum

Placing a number of photographs together on a page requires careful selection. These subjects work well together as they reflect the old and the new, the traditions and transitions, that are Japan.

Sailing the
South Pacific:

• Tonga

• Hawaii

Bon voyage and
smooth sailing!

*Materials:*

*Textured Vellum*      *Alphabet Stickers*
*Colored Construction Papers*      *Gold Crown Charm*
*Floral Die-cuts*      *Metallic Accents*

*Tonga*

Kings Throne, Tonga

Choose complementary colors to frame and accentuate the photograph.
The gold crown accent emphasizes the regalness of the event.

# Malo e lelei!

Use large lettering styles to emphasize the importance of the subject matter, or to identify a location visited.

## Materials:

*Dried Leaves*
*Toothpicks*
*Handmade Paper*
*Metallic Dragons*
*Gold Soldier Charms*
*Alphabet Stickers*

The textured leaf "paper" was created by weaving moistened toothpicks through large, green leaves and allowing them to dry flat. A variation of this technique could be sewing different swatches of material together with yarn or thread.

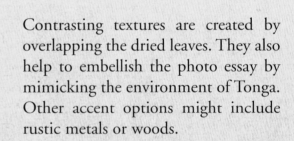

Contrasting textures are created by overlapping the dried leaves. They also help to embellish the photo essay by mimicking the environment of Tonga. Other accent options might include rustic metals or woods.

## Materials:

*Embossed Cardstock*
*Woven-bamboo Paper*
*Colored Rice Paper*
*Textured Pearlized Paper*
*Embossed Silver Leaves*
*Dragonfly Accent*
*Decorative Silver Bead*
*Small Twig*

Red floral-embossed cardstock echoes the design and color of the picture. Layering papers lifts up the photograph.

fresh (fresh) 1. recently made, grown 2. not spoiled 3. not tired, lively 4. new, recent 5. innocent

Utilizing dimensional items adds interest, especially when selected to enhance geographical phenomenon (i.e. the twig threaded through the bead). The metallic accents resemble carved stone like that found in the jungles of Tonga.

## Materials:
**Handwoven Paper**
**Handmade Paper**
**Textured Vellum**
**Fossilized Leaves**
**Acorns**
**Dried Seedpods**

The initial focus should be on the abundance of natural elements. The dried seedpods, fossilized leaves, and acorns are placed in a way that frames the pictures and "builds" up the composition, just like the hut in the picture was built. All of the organic materials mesh well together and create harmony.

The seedpods work well with the woven texture and naturalistic elements of the paper. Like the paper, all elements of these compositions have been woven together to form a pleasing whole. The organic feel also reflects the mood created by the photographs.

Small Village in Tonga

Tonga Home

## Materials:

*Scrapbook Papers*
*Cork Paper*
*Textured Vellum*
*Colored Cardstock*
*Small Twigs*
*Feather*

Placing the cork paper on top of the light blue cardstock and vellum is reminiscent of the canoe floating on the water. The way the twigs are attached parallels the way the paddles fall into the water.

*Fishing Canoe*

*Ancient Arch, Tonga*

The map motif of the scrapbook paper is fitting considering the locale and featured photograph. The picture is a jungle-like setting and it makes you feel a bit safer knowing that a map was included in the composition . . . just in case.

Balance has been achieved by using odd numbers of items in the design. For example, there are three photos, flowers, brads, and wired captions. Odd numbered presentations are more artistically effective.

# Aloha!

## A hawaiian Holiday

I loved Hawaii! It was so beautiful! I loved playing in the surf—I even saw a shark (ok, it was pretty small). We stayed in a beach house & visited the Polynesian cultural center. It was a great trip.

October 1979

Pearl Harbor

The personal journal response was printed on vellum, torn and placed atop another torn-edged dark background. This cloud-like effect is emphasized by the photograph at the base of the quote.

BY AIR MAIL
PAR AVION

Rec Aug 17 1854

POSTMASTER,

AIR MAIL
6¢
U.S. POSTAGE

County.

North American
Agenda:

• Nat'l Parks

• Arizona

• Nevada

• California

• Mexico

*Colored Cardstock*  *Decorative Buttons*
*Travel Brochures*  *String*
*Travel Postcards*  *Copper Brads*
*Colored Vellum*  *Adhesive Pop-dots*
*Scrapbook Paper*  *Walnut Ink*

Nat'l Parks

A pocket for travel brochures was created with colored vellum and brads. The torn paper, cover photo, and sewn-on button decorate the device and invite closer inspection of the travel brochures stored inside.

# Do not approach the wildlife.

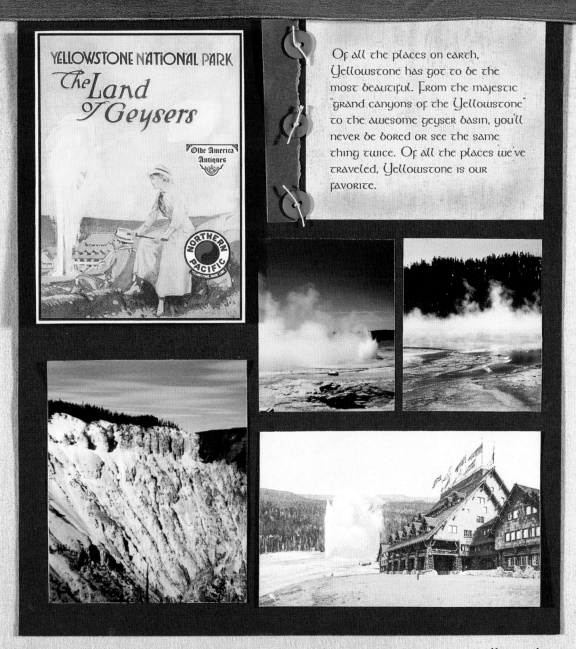

**YELLOWSTONE NATIONAL PARK**
*The Land of Geysers*

Olde America Antiques

NORTHERN PACIFIC

Of all the places on earth, Yellowstone has got to be the most beautiful. From the majestic "grand canyons of the Yellowstone" to the awesome geyser basin, you'll never be bored or see the same thing twice. Of all the places we've traveled, Yellowstone is our favorite.

The uniform placement of photographs on this page contrasts, ironically, to the spectacular variety of scenes and personal journal comment about the awesome diversity of Yellowstone.

## Materials:
*Embossed Cardstock*
*Patterned Paper*
*Cording & Trim Elements*
*Premade Spring Gift Tag*
*Assorted Ribbons & Rosettes*
*Various Beads*
*Clear Vellum*

The spring gift tag is purchased yet looks handmade. The photograph is a wordless statement about the highly anticipated pull of nature in that season; no time for camera posing!

Forrie & Winnie

Spring

How cute am I!

A variety of beads when used in combination creates character and unity. The flowers are composed of several different beads: the petals, leaves, and centers. Achieve interesting design by using variations of the same pattern. Dots are repeated in the embossed white paper, the polka-dot paper, and in the center of the floral accents. The ribbon rosettes have also been embellished with a central bead, tying them in with the overall design.

## Materials:
Hand-woven Paper
Handmade Papers
Wood-like Paper
Colored Cardstock
Fossilized Leaf
Cording & Trim Elements
Decorative Buttons & Beads

The woodgrained paper and fossilized leaf placed at the end of the branch extends the tree trunk outside the picture and enlarges the space.

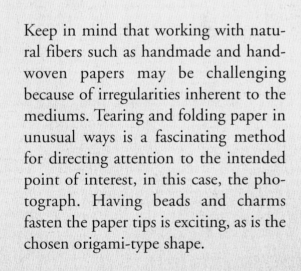

Keep in mind that working with natural fibers such as handmade and hand-woven papers may be challenging because of irregularities inherent to the mediums. Tearing and folding paper in unusual ways is a fascinating method for directing attention to the intended point of interest, in this case, the photograph. Having beads and charms fasten the paper tips is exciting, as is the chosen origami-type shape.

### Materials:
Colored Cardstocks
Handmade Paper
Corrugated Paper
Clear Vellum
Area Map
Colored Eyelets

The dramatic colors of Bryce Canyon are reflected in this selection of papers and accents. Torn background papers and borders mimic the geography. The single descriptive adjective is a perfect example of "less can be more." It also seems appropriate that the caption is handwritten in uneven lettering.

Beautiful

Bryce Canyon

Corrugated paper adds bumpy dimension to the rocky photographs. It is sometimes effective to include maps for pinpointing the exact locale, especially when the vacation spot is a frequently visited area and details are appreciated. Overlapping the picture above the map seems to lift the scene right up from below.

## Materials:

| | |
|---|---|
| Scrapbook Papers | Lettered Tags |
| Colored Cardstock | Twine & String |
| Camping Themed Die-cuts | Alphabet Beads |
| Photograph Frame | Colored Eyelets |
| Silver-edged Gift Tag | Copper Wire |
| Corrugated Paper | Copper Brads |

The clothesline caption design is very complementary to the layout of this page of campy photographs. The dated journal entry's shared feelings almost seem as a letter home, leading us to see the place as the author did.

This year for our annual camping trip, we went to Wyoming with the Nix family. The kids had a great time! They dubbed an old piece of wood in the pond "Frog Island" & spent most of their time searching for frogs. We had great meals, thanks to the two Barbra's excellent cooking. And of course, we roasted marshmallows and made smores. How fun it is to be outdoors!

July 2001

These pages utilize theme accents which may be purchased commercially. Hand-crafted objects tend to be more personal and unique, but usually require added time in their creation. Using manufactured materials conserves time while still producing a quality scrapbook page.

*Materials:*
**Textured Vellum**
**Geological Keepsakes**
**Product Tags**
**Magnifying Glass**

The folded product tags add spark and depth, along with interaction invites. Much like a pop-up book, the tags say "open me up" and the magnifying glass reiterates "explore and inspect." Don't be fooled into thinking that just children like this type of scrapbook page.

Scrapbook pages may be used as learning tools as well as for remembrance and record keeping. The product tags exhibited correspond with featured geological items purchased at the vacation site. The layout design, with the weight of the page to the left and use of white space to the right, suggests movement matching the action depicted on the tags.

**MANGANESE DENDRITE**

Multicolored ramifications resembling moss-like patterns over rock surfaces are known as Dendrites. Due to their structure (resembling fern plants and moss), in the past it was thought Dendrite to be vegetal remains. Dendrite formation is not due to remains of living organisms. The formation occurs because of the manganese and iron oxides deposits that penetrated along the rock-thin cracks. After the water evaporated the mineral deposits were left, giving the rock surface the appearance of an arborescence drawing.

## Materials:

*Handmade Paper*
*Colored Cardstock*
*Dinosaur Die-cut*
*Brochure Clippings*
*Souvenir Sticker*
*Amber Pieces*

Folding handmade paper around the page subtly softens straight edges and alludes to an opening or awakening, possibly that of the die-cut dinosaur. The opened mouth most certainly lends sound to the pattern. Again, factual information is pleasantly placed for non-threatening learning.

**DINOSAURS**

Dinosaurs are a group of animals related to birds and reptiles, extinct for more than 65 million years, that lived during the Mesozoic Era. Some had grotesque shapes, some had gigantic dimensions (some species reached 130 ft. in length), some others were no larger than chickens. They are considered to be among the largest animals that ever lived.

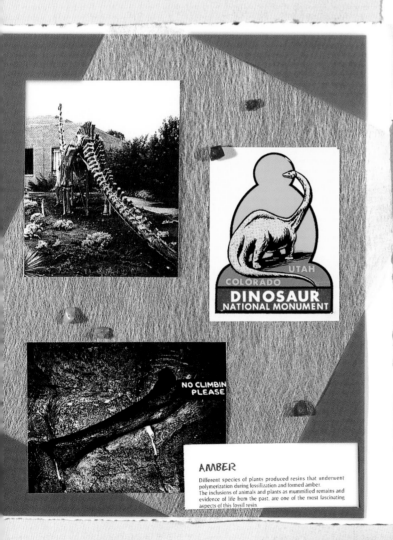

**UTAH**
**COLORADO**
**DINOSAUR**
**NATIONAL MONUMENT**

**NO CLIMBIN PLEASE**

**AMBER**

Different species of plants produced resins that underwent polymerization during fossilization and formed amber. The inclusions of animals and plants as mummified remains and evidence of life from the past, are one of the most fascinating aspects of this fossil resin.

Die-cuts relating to a layout's subject, offer easy variety. Those available for purchase range in size, color, and price, along with a wide spectrum of styles; from very simple shapes to delicate Victorian designs, from common renderings to artistic creations. The bony dinosaur shown here is very complex and perfectly matches the page's theme.

*Materials:*

**Colored Cardstock**  **Raffia**
**Clear Vellum**  **Gift Tag**
**Colored Thread**  **Colored Eyelets**
**Decorative Buttons**  **Foam-core**

*Arizona*

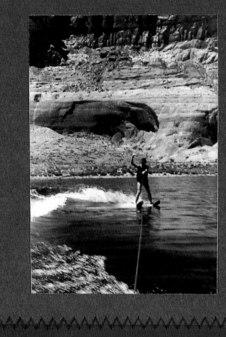

Creative foundations for pictures may include actually sewing blocks of colored cardstock together in a zig-zag manner. The photo corners have been fashioned by wrapping foam-core triangles with colored paper.

Lake
Powell

July
1981

Blue shades mimic the water and contrast the red rock formations, dramatically enhancing the featured landscapes. The awe inspiring yet very humbling surroundings correlate to feelings traditionally associated with the color blue.

## Materials:

*Woven-bamboo Paper*
*Textured Vellum*
*Iridescent Cardstock*
*Metallic Alphabet Rivets*
*Various Beads*
*Seashells*

The woven-bamboo paper is sand-like in texture and provides a perfect foundation for these compositions. The smaller beads glued around the Lake Powell caption suggest waves and the lines formed with the background papers seem to extend from the picture to define a houseboat setting.

Variations for captions might include mixing uppercase and lowercase riveted letters to create a playful tone; in this case, a successful reminder of the mood of this vacation. Intertwining beads together to form an exclamation point adds emphasis to a photograph or caption. Seashells form a stylish rod from which the photograph seems to dangle. The alphabet rivets are an unusual way to identify photographs.

## Materials:
### Cork Paper
### Colored Cardstock
### Copper Mesh
### Glass Shards

The translucence of water is mimicked in the addition of glass shards. Those, plus the crinkled copper mesh, install realism, dimension, and excitement. The chosen scenes are also an interesting combination; one picture with obvious action and a sense of discovery is placed askew, while the serene image is evenly aligned. Such subtle techniques display originality and encourage thoughtful perusal.

The rich earth tones of the photographs displayed inspired the organic accent materials and the grainy, cork backdrop. Of special interest is the layout design of the purplish cardstock at dramatic angle to the brown. This technique draws attention to similar contrasts in the photographs; sharp lines and edges of rocks suddenly meeting vivid water.

*Materials:*

*Scrapbook Papers*
*Paint Swatches*
*Dragonfly Stickers*
*Miniature Wire Hangers*
*Beach Towel Accents*
*Floral Die-cuts*

Unique photo corners can be made by cutting slits into paint sample swatches; it's a simple and inexpensive way to decorate a page since the swatches are free. Using corners to hold photographs on the page eliminates the need for adhesives and allows for photographs to be changed occasionally.

Surprises are created by placing items within a page design that seem incongruous at first glance and, therefore, solicit further inspection and analysis. The towel accents hanging above the photograph of the boat, and the large dragonfly stickers hovering below, illustrate this technique. Also effective for this layout are the horizontal strips of color which aptly signify the shore and cliffs surrounding the lake.

## Materials:
*Colored Cardstock*
*Handmade Paper*
*Miniature Gift Tags*
*Colored Thread*
*Walnut Ink*
*Carved Stone Accents*

Choosing verbs and adjectives in conjunction with the pictures, simplifies the scenes and adds to the fun. Placing each letter on a miniature gift tag makes them appear as small, flat stones. The attached strings which gather at the very edge of the page seem to counter the impossibility of pulling back a skipping thrill.

*Talk about your mud pie !*
*Jerad*

*The famous rock skipper at Lake Powell*
*ADAM*

An imaginative technique to create the stone-like appearance of age or weathering is to lightly brush walnut-colored ink over the miniature tags, foundation paper, matting, or even the photograph itself. The result is the appearance of light sand and an extension of the action in the pictures. Repeat brushing over the handwritten captions adds to the artistic balance of the composition.

*Materials:*

Handpainted Paper      Assorted Ribbons
Textured Tissue Paper      Rosebud Trim
Heart Accents      Alphabet Stickers

*Nevada*

*Mr. & Mrs. Rhinehart*
*2·0·0·1*

Placing the close-up photograph near the top, above the layers of paper, ribbon, caption and ruffling, is artistically much like a tiered wedding cake. The handwritten name and date personalizes the whole.

# Chapel of Love!

RENO

*Love*   *Love*

DANCE

Adjacent to any wedding, one finds ribbons, tissue paper, and hearts. Using the same items as accents on a page with that theme makes us participants in the celebration. Horizontal lines express longevity and the soft yellow tones add femininity.

**Materials:**
Patterned Vellum
Colored Cardstock
Silver Charms
Silver String Beads
Sheer Ribbon
White Rice
Wire Lettering
Heart Accent

When attaching metal or wire objects, such as charms, string beads, and wire letters, use a special metal glue to ensure permanent adhesion.

Reno

Chad

The Rhinehart Men

Love

dream

Forrest

Wedding flowers

2000

The confetti-print vellum and scattered rice communicate celebration. The heart accent placed at the top of the page, is central to the focus, as is the joyful posing of the participants beneath it. The extension of beads from edge to edge symbolizes the continuity and longevity inherent in the theme of marriage.

## Materials:

*Patterned Paper*
*Embossed Vellum*
*Sheer Pom-pom Ribbon*
*Alphabet Stickers*
*Butterfly Accents*
*Shoe Stickers*
*Colored Cardstock*
*Clear Heart Stickers*

The translucent vellum, embossed with flowers and calligraphy, lends formality and elegance to the occasion featured. The butterfly accents and casual alignment of the stickers forming the names hint at the fluttery nerves associated with a special day such as this.

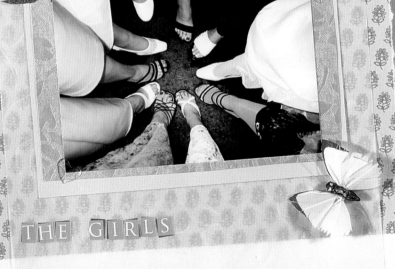

The shoes form an implied circle which is offset by the lines of the ribbon. An element of fun is added by the inclusion of the shoe stickers. They echo the subject of the photograph, extending the impact of the image onto the page. Their specific placement also injects motion into a static scene.

## Materials:

| | | |
|---|---|---|
| Embossed Borders & Corners | Fossilized Leaves | Raised Pear Stamp |
| Decorative Buttons | Feather | Raised Heart Stamp |
| Various Beads | Fabric Mesh | Carved Stone Accent |
| Silver Picture Frame | Silk Ribbon | String |
| Embossed Cardstock | Floral Die-cuts | Walnut Ink |
| Gift Tags | Alphabet Stickers | Copper Wire |

Framing helps to link one page to the next. This may also be accomplished with ribbons, buttons, beads, and tags used on both layouts, as seen here. Such pages can be purely decorative, displayed as a means of artistic expression. The artist chose to have the photograph as a small central scene, secondary to the larger surrounding accents.

*Materials:*

Silk Ribbons  
Decorative Buttons & Beads  
Silver Edged Gift Tag  
Textured Note-card  
Starfish & Seashells  

Wire Lettering  
Small Twig  
Silver Vellum  
Silver Wire  
Colored Thread

*California*

*mother*

Natural, intriguing artifacts, unusual in structure, can be fascinating additions to compositions. The items here are visually interesting and add to the scene, as if they could have been found on the visited shore.

# California dreamin'!

"The matriarchs sit in their places,
unmoved, transparent,
like ships on a sea,
observing the terrorist waves.

Where do they come from,
Where to go?
They move out of corners,
from the quick of our lives."
Pablo Neruda

The artistic design of this page draws in even the most casual observer. Every element of the composition connects to the wonderful photograph and stirring quote. The mood whispers peaceful observation.

### Materials:

*Silk Ribbon*
*Silver Eyelet Lettering*
*Silver Eyelets*
*Sheer Fabric Mesh*
*Sand Dollar & Seashells*
*Decorative Buttons & Beads*
*Feathers*

These two pages form a combined composition, established with the titled play on words. The silk ribbon draws the eye across both scenes. An informal alternative to photograph corners, glues, tapes, or other adhesive devices are eyelets. Remember, though, that they have an unattractive backside.

Chad, moss cove
1980

Don't be afraid of layering items on top of your photographs or cropping them to eliminate unnecessary elements. The placement of a sheer fabric mesh atop the picture offers a gritty sense of the beach and the boys.

## Materials:

Silk Ribbons

Silver Eyelets

Picture Mat

Gift Box Lid

Safety Pin

Silver Eyelet Lettering

Fan-folded Fabric

Starfish & Seashells

Decorative Buttons & Beads

Ship In A Bottle Sticker

A thick picture mat, the same color as the foundation paper, allows shadows to frame the photograph. At first glance the picture seems too small for the page, but the intended message becomes clearer with study. It's a huge ocean, and he's a very small part of the frothy surf.

Chad Boogie Boarding - the surf

Chad

Shadow boxes can easily be made from gift box lids of assorted sizes. As seen below, they highlight the action and personality of the photographs and provide for inclusion of actual souvenirs and memorabilia.

Moss Cove with Granny & Papa

Jerad

*Materials:*

Scrapbook Paper      Colored Wire
Travel Keepsakes      Assorted Ribbons
Gift Tag      Sandal Charm
Hot Tamale & Sun Die-cuts      Photo Corners
Decorative Leaf Buttons      Gold Brads

The bright and vibrant colors that are Mexico are represented here. Juxtaposed to the rapid pace of the tones, is the relaxing rhythm within the photographs.

Actually sewing things onto a scrapbook page is a graphic technique. The thin, colored wire was manipulated to spell Mexico and is sewn into the paper. It was also used as the sun's central spiral on the previous page.

*Materials:*
*Scrapbook Papers*
*Alphabet Stickers*
*Kite Accents*
*Gold Hinge & Clasp*
*Foam-core*
*Rubber Stamp of Sun*
*Twine & Raffia*

This unusual, photograph-free page has artistic intent. The faux travel journal was created by wrapping scrapbook paper around foam-core board and adding hinges and a clasp. The message is open for interpretation.

mexico

cabo

san Lucas

Mounting photographs on foam-core lifts them off the page and towards you. Raising elements up off the page in varying heights adds variety and creates shadows for creative design.

*Scrapbook Papers*
*Handmade Paper*
*Floral Die-cuts*
*Decorative Buttons*
*Alphabet Stickers*
*Fabric Mesh*
*Postcard Stickers*

Large flowers recreate the life and color that is associated with this vacation destination. The simple die-cut shapes have been enhanced by the placement of contrasting buttons glued on as centers. They add excitement, especially mounted slightly overlapping the photographs, suggesting we enter the scene through them.

Embellishments may be themed to reiterate any aspect of the original experience which the artist wants to remember or explain. For example, this layout features postcard stickers and a handwritten message saying "wish you were here." The design is straightforward, obvious in intent and message, as opposed to some pages which are significantly symbolic and thought-provoking. Inclusion of such diverse compositions in a collection holds interest throughout the entire album.

# About The Author

Susan Ure, a native of Washington and former owner of the gift shop, FLORIBUNDA, has lived the past 30 years in Salt Lake City, Utah. She has three sons, six grandchildren, and resides with her husband and two dogs in the foothills overlooking the city.

Even at a very young age she loved designing and arranging things, even moving and revamping the furnishings and decor of her family's home. Through the years, Susan's talent for decorating has become a polished and distinctive style that has inspired many clients, friends, and family.

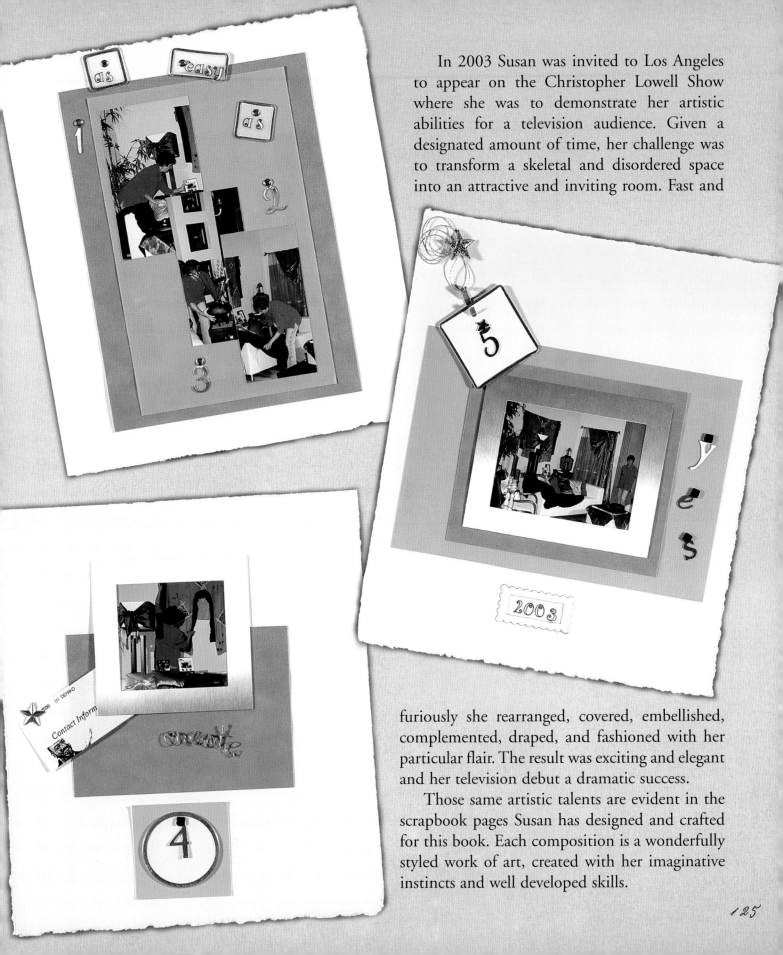

In 2003 Susan was invited to Los Angeles to appear on the Christopher Lowell Show where she was to demonstrate her artistic abilities for a television audience. Given a designated amount of time, her challenge was to transform a skeletal and disordered space into an attractive and inviting room. Fast and furiously she rearranged, covered, embellished, complemented, draped, and fashioned with her particular flair. The result was exciting and elegant and her television debut a dramatic success.

Those same artistic talents are evident in the scrapbook pages Susan has designed and crafted for this book. Each composition is a wonderfully styled work of art, created with her imaginative instincts and well developed skills.

# Acknowledgments

Special thanks and appreciation to:

My friend Jo for trusting in my creativity and inviting me to do this book.

Cathy Brammwell and Katie Ure for their elegant penmanship.

Paige Hill for providing alternate examples of scrapbook pages.

Jayne Johnson and Melissa Maynard for their eloquent and insightful writings.

Marilyn Goff and Kim Taylor for their hard work and attention to detail.

You say how big?

## Metric Equivalency Chart

mm-millimeters  cm-centimeters
inches to millimeters and centimeters

| inches | mm | cm | inches | cm | inches | cm |
|---|---|---|---|---|---|---|
| ⅛ | 3 | 0.3 | 9 | 22.9 | 30 | 76.2 |
| ¼ | 6 | 0.6 | 10 | 25.4 | 31 | 78.7 |
| ½ | 13 | 1.3 | 12 | 30.5 | 33 | 83.8 |
| ⅝ | 16 | 1.6 | 13 | 33.0 | 34 | 86.4 |
| ¾ | 19 | 1.9 | 14 | 35.6 | 35 | 88.9 |
| ⅞ | 22 | 2.2 | 15 | 38.1 | 36 | 91.4 |
| 1 | 25 | 2.5 | 16 | 40.6 | 37 | 94.0 |
| 1¼ | 32 | 3.2 | 17 | 43.2 | 38 | 96.5 |
| 1½ | 38 | 3.8 | 18 | 45.7 | 39 | 99.1 |
| 1¾ | 44 | 4.4 | 19 | 48.3 | 40 | 101.6 |
| 2 | 51 | 5.1 | 20 | 50.8 | 41 | 104.1 |
| 2½ | 64 | 6.4 | 21 | 53.3 | 42 | 106.7 |
| 3 | 76 | 7.6 | 22 | 55.9 | 43 | 109.2 |
| 3½ | 89 | 8.9 | 23 | 58.4 | 44 | 111.8 |
| 4 | 102 | 10.2 | 24 | 61.0 | 45 | 114.3 |
| 4½ | 114 | 11.4 | 25 | 63.5 | 46 | 116.8 |
| 5 | 127 | 12.7 | 26 | 66.0 | 47 | 119.4 |
| 6 | 152 | 15.2 | 27 | 68.6 | 48 | 121.9 |
| 7 | 178 | 17.8 | 28 | 71.1 | 49 | 124.5 |
| 8 | 203 | 20.3 | 29 | 73.7 | 50 | 127.0 |

# Index